REJECTING

THE SPIRIT OF

REJECTION

Dr. Vivian Carroll, Ph. D.

NOUS
MASS
MEDIA

REJECTING THE SPIRIT OF REJECTION

Carroll Enterprise, LLC
137 Danbury Rd.
New Milford, CT 06776

ISBN-13: 978-1973936503
ISBN-10: 197393650X
Printed in the United States of America
Copyright © 2017 Dr. Vivian Carroll, Ph. D.

Graphics: VividArts *By Jamel*
info@vividartsbyjamel.com

Nous Mass Media
9494 Humble Westfield Rd. #432
Humble, Texas 77338
www.nousmassmedia.com

CONTENTS

DEDICATION   5
ACKNOWLEDGMENTS   6
PRELUDE 8
WHAT IS THE SPIRIT OF REJECTION?   11
TYPES OF REJECTION   15
ROOT CAUSES OF REJECTION   30
HOW JESUS WAS REJECTED   34
OVERCOMING REJECTION
PRAYER OF DELIVERANCE FROM THE
SPIRIT OF REJECTION   39

DEDICATION

Rejecting the Spirit of Rejection is dedicated to EVERYONE, who has ever experienced the spirit of rejection.

It is my prayer that after reading this book you will accept God's unconditional love that He offers you.

"For God so loved the world that HE gave HIS only begotten son, that whosoever believeth in HIM should not perish, but have everlasting life." John 3:16.

ACKNOWLEDGMENTS

To my Heavenly Father, Jesus Christ, His Son, our Savior, and Holy Spirit, our Comforter, and Wonderful Counselor: I give you all the honor and all the glory for my salvation, deliverance, and healing. *"I shall not die, but live, and declare the works of the Lord"*, (Psalm 118:17).

To my husband Apostle Stanley Carroll: We had no idea what God was up to when He ordained our marriage covenant. Twenty-five years later, our journey is still unfolding and He has preserved us for such a time as this. I appreciate the revelation knowledge you have imparted to me through the years. It has blessed my walk with the Lord. I Love you.

To our sons Jahrell and Jamel: It is amazing to witness the accomplishments you are making and I know your personal acceptance of Jesus Christ as Lord in your lives, has made the difference. We are proud of you and love you both dearly.

To my parents Louis and Pernell Dykes: I appreciate your sacrifice to educate me. It has really paid off.

To my sister Linda Matthews: Thanks for the times we spent as kids reading and talking about books. I became a lover of books.

To Dr. Lovella Mogere: Thank you for hearing God's heartbeat and helping me to make my dream of writing this book come true.

To Apostle Mary Lewis: Thank you for your teaching and sharing your God-given wisdom. My life has forever been impacted.

PRELUDE

The spirit of rejection is a destructive, evil spirit. It is the enemy of our soul, satan, that invades the countless lives of many people every single day! Behind the scenes, this deceiver uses people and situations to go after his prey.

The spirit of rejection is prevalent in every ethnic culture, race, religion, gender, and age group. It has no limitations or boundaries! Many may not know that they are being or have been a victim.

To enlighten you, the spirit of rejection is in total opposition to the perfect will of God for your life, purpose, and destiny. Its primary objective is to afflict and torment its victims with negative emotions of insignificance, low-self-estimation, and worthlessness.

Feelings of being unaccepted, unappreciated, unrecognized, and unloved, can be a constant bombardment to one's soul, over and over again until this vicious cycle has stopped. In addition, its victims feel depressed, defeated, degenerated denounced, and devalued. They appear to have the inability to fit the social norms and status quo at hand.

The spirit of rejection is manifested when a parent favors one child over another, when a teenager is ostracized by his peers at school or a couple is going through a divorce, and when a person did not qualify for a particular job, etc. These scenarios are just examples to name a few.

The question may be asked what is the difference between rejection and abandonment? Do they go hand in hand? For clarity, abandonment is rejection inflicted upon an individual that he knows or recognizes well. Whether it be a family member, friend, neighbor, or co-worker, etc., it can be quite devastating, to say the least! The spirit of rejection attempted to destroy me from the onset of conception in the womb and since then, I have encountered this spirit on multiple occasions, throughout my entire life!

Because of my love relationship with Jesus Christ, my Lord, and Savior, I am able to reject the spirit of rejection and walk in victory. It's my heartfelt prayer that after reading this book, you will accept the love of Jesus and do the same.

1

WHAT IS THE SPIRIT OF REJECTION?

The spirit of rejection is an evil spirit from our adversary, satan, that attempts to afflict, torment, plague and ultimately destroy us in order to prevent us from fulfilling our divine purpose that God has designed for us, before the foundation of this world. Rejection influences someone to experience or undergo a feeling of being unloved, unwanted, unimportant, and insignificant. It is the refusal to be accepted by someone.

Sometimes we can have goals, dreams, ideas, and aspirations that we share with loved ones and friends. Our expectation for relaying them to our loved ones and friends is so we would get positive feedback, encouragement, affirmations, and a little pat on the back that would stimulate us to move forward to achieve and accomplish great things in life. Instead, a negative feedback or gesture may hit us unexpectedly in the face!

It can really come across as a condescending put-down, mocking, debilitating spirit. You wished you would have remained silent and kept your visions and dreams to yourself! When you are excited and full of hope and you share it with the wrong people, it is almost as if your lips have invited a beating! To be told you are incapable of doing this, that, or the other, can be very discouraging. What about when you are told a list of reasons why the odds are against you for so many foolish reasons? It is actually the voice of a person who will never get out the boat!

Foster children and orphans experience parental rejection and abandonment every single day, while awaiting loveable caretakers to rescue them to a safe haven call home. Just imagine the pain and agony in their hearts. Another case of rejection and abandonment occurs when a parent selects one of the children as the favorite, and it is very obvious who the rejected child is because he goes unnoticed and unattended in that dysfunctional home. (See chapter 2 about parental rejection).

An unfaithful spouse causes the other spouse to suffer and feel emotionally abused, neglected, rejected and abandoned. Time for healing and restoration is needed in order for this marital relationship to even survive. Prayer and marriage counseling can be a blessing for starters.

Rejection ignored can really lead to a very unhealthy, unfruitful life if it is not dealt with. Below is a list of some emotional wounds that can develop:

Un-forgiveness	Fear
Bitterness	Worry
Loneliness	Depression
Isolation	Paranoia
Guilt	Perfectionism
Shame	Resentment
Insecurity	Bipolar
Inferiority	Mental illness
Suicide	Schizophrenia

It is very imperative to reject the spirit of rejection and not allow it to penetrate and invade your soul. It opens doors to bigger problems as you can see from the list above. I have counseled adults who had unfulfilled and very wounded lives because they were rejected in childhood. You cannot heal a thing if you continue to deny it exists.

2

TYPES OF REJECTION

Fear is False Evidence Appearing Real! Statistically, it has a major impact on millions of lives every day. Fear has the ability to cripple you, and ultimately paralyze you if you don't get from under it! The fear of rejection can grip you and disable you from moving forward and succeeding in every area of your life. Where there is an opportunity for progress, growth, advancement, and achievement, the fear of rejection will more than likely, raise its ugly head. This fear is being afraid that someone will not accept you and your uniqueness or even appreciate the way you perform a particular task.

The fear of rejection can infuse you with unfavorable thoughts of inferiority, insecurity, and inadequacy. It disrupts a positive overall view of oneself. For example, instead of a person having the courage, the tenacity, and the wherewithal to pursue a job interview, a person may very suddenly and anxiously become overwhelmed with self-doubt and begin thinking of the idea not to maintain the appointment, "after all, he rationalizes, the other candidate is probably more qualified and will get the job anyway".

The fear of rejection seeks to deter someone from events like auditioning for a major motion picture, getting dressed for a blind date, entering college for the first time, or from the grand opening of a very lucrative business just an hour before. While we may have a wonderful God-given vision and plan for our lives, we must be on the lookout for self-sabotaging thoughts!

To overcome the fear of rejection:

1. You have to be willing to be a risk taker and be willing to launch your creativity at all costs.
2. Be optimistic about new, innovative ideas and goals. Live on the cutting edge with expectation.

3. You have to be confident enough and assured enough that your gift will make room for you. (Proverbs 18:16)
4. Never attempt to be a people-pleaser. In the long run, you will get exhausted and burned out! Just focus on what you are supposed to be accomplishing and seek to maximize your potential.

Sometimes people battle the fear of rejection so bad until they start rejecting others first. A groom calls off the wedding because he felt his in-laws desired someone more affluent. A young lady turns down a singing contest for fear of being disqualified. A student turned down a peer mentorship program because of her broken English. A woman refused a seventy percent discount for a gym membership across the street because she would noticeably be among the few senior attendees in this new establishment.

In retrospect of the cases I just previously mentioned, many healthy, productive relationships get sabotaged with the toxic ones, all because they were dominated by the fear of rejection. Remember, For God hath not given us the spirit of fear; but of power, and of love, and of a sound mind. (2 Timothy 1:7, KJV).

I will never forget reading about a high profile person that failed to uphold his standard of moral character and integrity, and as a result, he was fired from his position as a great leader. It was concluded that while he had to endure public shame, disgrace, and embarrassment, he was able to walk away, holding his head up high.

Why was this possible? This man endured societal rejection, while receiving parental, unconditional love and acceptance. This caused him to walk away with his head up in spite of the great loss of his reputation and honor. What if this man, who had in fact, pleaded guilty, had undergone not only societal rejection, but parental rejection on top of everything else? He may have buried his head in endless reproach, rebuke, guilt, shame and scorn. Having his parents demonstrate unconditional love and acceptance at probably the most humiliating and degrading time in his life, may have taken some of the edge off the pain

and suffering of a great reputation gone completely
sour! "A hard pill to swallow", is an understatement.

PARENTAL REJECTION

It has been said that parental rejection, out of all
the kinds of rejection one can experience, is by far the
worst and the most devastating. Parental rejection is
when your own parent(s) reject you, or refuse to accept
you, for whatever reason. Simply put and worth
repeating, this rejection is abandonment because you
know the person who has rejected you all to well! This
really hurts.

Research has stated, while rejection can be very
traumatic and devastating, from both parents, rejection
from the father can do greater damage. The father's
role is to govern, guard, provide and affirm his
children. He is supposed to pass on the positive nature
and identity to his legacy. When a young boy is
affirmed and called, "Champion" and a young girl is
called, "Princess" by their father, they can find

themselves walking through life's journey with approval, confidence, and a healthy self-image. Regardless of race, culture, gender, economic status, religion, parental rejection causes emotional, chronic wounds of low self-estimation, self-doubt, anxiety, insecurity, and depression, which can be long-term throughout adulthood.

Victims of parental rejection may become angry, aggressive, and hostile towards others if it is not addressed. Children that have experienced parental rejection have the tendency to become adults who lack strong, trusting relationships and wholesome communication skills. I have watched children suffer from parental rejection because their parents were overwhelmed and frustrated single moms, their parents were filing for a divorce, or there were just too many children in the household to give each child undivided attention. In my opinion, fatherless homes have hurt many children to the core. It affects one generation after another.

I am suggesting that people come to terms with whether they have experienced parental rejection and to start the healing process by forgiving their parents, which means to release them and the pain they caused, and truly strive hard to let go. You can never move forward in continuous cycles of deadly emotions.

Forgiveness is very good for the souls of wounded hearts. Oftentimes the one(s) who hurt you, may not even realize the severe damage they have done, or they are no longer alive to repent about it. Psalm 27:10 comforts by saying, *"When my father and my mother forsake me, then the Lord will take me up.*

PERCEIVED REJECTION

Perceived rejection is when a person interprets a particular act done towards him as rejection, when in fact, that's not really the case at all; it is further from the truth. A person, for example, could be staring at another person for a pretty lengthy time on a crowded train and it may feel as though the person staring is taking an x-ray of his entire body.

Now the individual that is being stared at, is feeling quite uncomfortable and anxious about the situation. The initial thoughts are negative and it appears that the person staring has some sort of disdain in his heart and may seek to do some type of harm. The train becomes uncrowded and the person that was staring politely comes over, introduces himself and proceeds to explain that he was at a school reunion and noticed his face from the yearbook. The gentleman, and that he was, even addressed him by his actual name with confidence. The bottom line is, the person that was staring had recognized the right person, although his motives, unbeknownst to the other gentleman, may have appeared somewhat suspicious.

I AM GUILTY OF PERCEIVING REJECTION

Sometimes I had to realize that I may have allowed an erroneous thought to creep in while engaged in conversation with someone. That very thought caused me to feel rejected. Notice I said, "feel". Emotions can get us in trouble. The individual's motivation may have been totally contrary to what I was feeling. It is best to guard your thoughts, get the facts, and not assume. I have made the decision not to rely on a text message, an email, or second hand information. I'd rather adhere to audible communication from the other party for clarity.

When I am hosting women conferences and I am dealing with the subject of rejection, I may relay to the women that what they perceive as rejection from their husbands may not be that at all. What makes it so bad, the husbands are often not even aware of it!
Very early on in my marriage, I learned that men used one or two sides of their brain at a time, and women are able to use four sides of their brain at a time, which makes us very good at multi-tasking. Men on the other hand, compartmentalize events and can handle one or two tasks at a time. I discovered that when I went downstairs, and found my husband enjoying the game on television, he was not rejecting me or ignoring me, he was just watching the game and having a ball! If I was sports-oriented, I would have been enjoying it too!

Recently, an acquaintance of mine gave me a compliment and I felt I had reciprocated it in a kind way, but she thought my response was a reprimand.

Although I was a bit surprised, thinking that there was clarity in my communication, I realized I was just a phone call away, and so I resolved the perceived rejection that was in effect. People who have experienced the spirit of rejection deal with perceived rejection as well and they have the tendency to run away with it. Again, it is best to get the facts rather than being led by the emotions and assumptions. You can save yourself a lot of wasted time and energy from paranoia.

SELF-REJECTION

What would cause a person to reject the themselves? This occurs when a person develops a dislike for who they are and everything about themselves. This deadly emotion can become so rotten to the core and cause self-hate. How much can you achieve and accomplish in this life without loving yourself unconditionally?

It is becoming more and more prevalent that people are turning on themselves and ending their lives by committing suicide. I have met and counseled men and women who hated themselves. They are often depressed, withdrawn from social interaction, and engulfed in guilt, shame, and defeat. They also find it very hard to let go of ill-spoken words that were spoken over them.

When a person rejects himself, he can no longer see a wonderful purpose in his total existence. Not loving and accepting yourself can send a message that you do not forgive yourself for having done something wrong. Failures, misfortunes, mistreatments, inability to cope with life's heavy burdens, and comparing oneself to others that are successful, can cause a person to proceed down a spiral staircase in his life. Without seeking help, self-rejection can lead to an unwanted disaster. Jeremiah 29:11 KJV, states, *"For I know the thoughts that I think toward you, saith the Lord, thoughts of peace, and not of evil, to give you an expected end"*.

SOCIAL REJECTION

When I was in sixth grade I had the worst gym class of my life! This particular day, we were given free time to play our individual games. The boys in my class had chosen to play basketball on one side of the gym, while the girls played jump rope on the other side of the gym. I didn't get an opportunity to play at all. I don't recall where the gym teacher was, but I know he wasn't present to control the situation and return my sneaker. My mom and dad had purchased these inexpensive sneakers for me and they weren't the latest style the kids were wearing at that time. I didn't like them either, but what could I do about it? To the boys in my class, my sneakers became the brunt of many jokes. As a result, I found myself spending the entire gym period chasing the boys, trying to retrieve my sneaker. They had used it to throw it into the basketball hoop and they deliberately ignored my request to stop. They really had fun at my expense! Sometimes, kids can be so cruel in school. Nowadays it's worse. Your life may be on the line.

That day at school I had experienced the shame and embarrassment of social rejection. This occurs when an individual, (just as myself that day) is deliberately, intentionally, excluded from social relationships or social interaction. A person can be rejected by an individual or an entire group of people. This kind of rejection is active if bullying, teasing, ridiculing and ostracizing someone is taking place. Social rejection can be passive if someone is ignored by being given the "cold shoulder" or given the "silent treatment". Some rejection is inevitably part of human life, nevertheless, it can pose a problem when it becomes a long-term issue.

There are some people who are not great in handling social rejection. They:

1) Decided that their self-image is depended upon whether or not they can become more socially successful. Every rejection, mistake or setback, hits them deep in their core, and they feel worthless.

2) Are ready to give up and throw in the towel because they have been rejected" one time too many", and they really can't be subjected to much more.

3) May become so resentful and bitter that the more they are rejected, the more they tend to overgeneralize and develop a negative attitude towards an entire category of people, they determined have shunned them. As a defense mechanism, they have discontinued friendship relations.

On the other hand, there are some victims of social rejection that have overcome this evil and have a much easier time coping and living their life.
Well, what's their secret? What's their method to this madness you may ask?
Certainly victims of social rejection had to overcome with a measure of optimism:

1) They are adamant about changing their attitude towards it and achieving success.

2) They are not totally immune from the sting of rejection, but they are determined to face it head on. They depend on their confidence and comfort in God to hold on.

3) They have been rejected and have regretfully made a lot of mistakes in their past, and are now determined to move forward with positive expectations.

4) They know and are fully aware that rejection is part of the process of trying to form a social life. They think long-term, and focus on what their end goals are.

5) Lastly, they realize everyone gets rejected at some point or another; even self-assured, astute, prestigious, good looking people who seem to have it all together.

3

ROOT CAUSES OF REJECTION

While we know the enemy has attempted to mastermind the spirit of rejection and release it upon the lives of many individuals as his prey, we can now seize the opportunity to observe the strategies he uses to maneuver and take control. First of all, there are several root causes of the rejection that we need to identify. Like seeds, these root causes are planted and major damage results in the spiritual, emotional, mental, physical, and social lives of others.

The manner and timing of conception in a mother's womb is very crucial. An unwanted pregnancy can occur due to a teenage pregnancy, an attempted abortion, a financial crisis, poor health, or even a rape.

As a result, the unborn baby may experience emotional neglect and trauma in the womb, instead of unconditional love, affection, acceptance and a warm and nurturing environment.

Delivery can be very long and tedious, causing an increase in the fear of death, anxiety, and worry. Inevitably, the baby is affected by what the mother goes through, whether positive or negative. Babies also wind up lethargic, weak and frail, with low birth rate because the mother is a substance abuser of some sort. Oftentimes the necessity of prenatal care is obsolete. When a baby does not experience early maternal bonding and nurturing from the mother, the prolonged absence and separation cause rejection, abandonment, a lack of trust , security, and a lack of dependency for love and care. Unfortunately, development of their own identity and their overall makeup is often delayed long term and detriment is inevitable.

From my relationships or encounters with women who have been adopted, they have often shared with me their profound feelings of rejection and abandonment even though their adoptive parents may have given them a very loving and nurturing home environment. They often wonder why their biological parents abandoned them in the first place. Who are they? What do they look like? Will they ever meet them face to face? It all remains as unanswered questions in their minds.

Root causes of rejection can also stem from a dysfunctional home, where there is constant marital discord, strife, physical, mental, and emotional abuse. The standards of love are established by these depressing conditions. Some children seldom recall hearing kind or encouraging words. Instead, they can recall being cursed at, ridiculed, or put down in such a very harsh condescending manner, that left them so wounded, lost, and broken. Verbal abuse can be just as bad as physical abuse!

For the physically abused child, there is immediate fear, confusion, and emotional misplacement. This rejection produces rebellion, anger, bitterness, rage, depression, and thoughts of revenge towards the "so-called" parent role model. A child that has been subjected to sexual abuse in the home, develops an inability to open up and communicate with people. The trauma causes a lack of trust and respect especially towards authority figures because he has been violated in an unnatural way.

There are many people who have experienced rejection and abuse from childhood and wind up as adults with unresolved emotional wounds that have never healed. These wounds grow and fester into bitterness, envy, jealousy, un-forgiveness, anger, and blaming God. These very negative strongholds are deadly emotional systems that invade the person's spirit, soul, and body and keep them bound for long periods of time. Oftentimes, there is a history of repeat cycles because victims become abusers themselves when these issues are not dealt with. In my opinion, suppressing any bad event in one's life is one of the worst things a person can do. The injury is never going to go away. It will resurface again, often worse than before. It is important to note that rejection fosters rebellion, which leads to a series of more problems as mentioned in chapter 1.

4

HOW JESUS WAS REJECTED

About a year ago, the spirit of rejection began to invade my peace. So, I began to talk to the Lord about it as I prayed and marched around my dining room table, quoting scriptures that tell me otherwise. I was not going to allow this spirit to accompany me for dinner! No doom and gloom or pity party in my presence! I determined in my spirit, soul, and body, enough was enough!

If I would have entertained it, it would have lingered and there would have been a depressing opportunity to go inward and focus on myself. So I continued in prayer until my peace was restored. Then a little while later the Lord spoke and reminded me,

"Jesus was rejected". When I heard this, immediately He led me to refocus on Him, our Lord and Savior. The scripture records in Isaiah 53:3 KJV, *"He is despised and rejected of men; a man of sorrows, and acquainted with grief: and we hid as it were our faces from him; he was despised, and we esteemed him not"*. Jesus became a substitute for sin for us; He became a sacrificial lamb that we might receive salvation and eternal life. He hung on a tree so that we would escape the penalty of death. He was emotionally wounded that we might receive emotional healing. He spent three days in hell so that we would victoriously be able to overcome the powers of darkness. He suffered thirty-nine stripes so that we would be physically healed. He was severely bruised and rejected so that we would be freed from emotional bruises of rejection.

Jesus was rejected during conception in the womb and throughout HIS entire life on earth. Jesus' birth and childhood had a stigma attached to it. Being born of the Virgin Mary, many thought Jesus was an illegitimate child. Jesus' parents had to take him and flee from King Herod who sought to kill him. Chief priests, scribes, and Pharisees questioned Jesus' identity on several occasions. Spiritual leaders accused him of being demon possessed. His so – called friends Peter and Judas, denied and betrayed him publicly. Mark 6:4 KJV, records the words of Jesus: "A prophet is not without honor, but in his own country, and among his own kin, and in his own house". Jesus could not perform mighty works of deliverance and healing in his very own hometown because he was reduced to just a plain old carpenter's son! He was not respected and placed in high regard as the Son of God, in the highest authority with dominion, and power. "He came unto His own, and His own received Him not", (John 1:11 KJV). The local, common people put Jesus on equal, familiar plain with them. Barabbas, a notorious prisoner, was released, but Jesus was falsely accused, mocked, scorned, spat upon, disfigured and violently beaten to death.

Ultimately, it was the plan of salvation that He would bare the humiliation and shame so you and I could live. As an overcomer in Christ Jesus, I became determined to do the rejecting instead and speak life into the very fiber of my being. I chose to accept my Heavenly Father's love and the power of HIS word.

Psalm 107:20 KJV: *He sent HIS word and healed them, and delivered them from their destructions.*

Psalm 118:17 KJV: *I shall not die, but live, and declare the works of the Lord.*

Psalm 139:13, 14 KJV: *For thou hast possessed my reins: thou hast covered me in my mother's womb. I will praise thee; for I am fearfully and wonderfully made: marvelous are thy works; and that my soul knoweth right well.*

HIS deliverance, healing, and restoration has blessed my soul and drawn me even closer to HIM in HIS presence. I praise HIM, worship HIM, and give HIM all the honor and all the glory! I rejoice about it! Now, I encourage you to embark on this wonderful, intimate, journey of freedom that is only found in HIM....

5

OVERCOMING REJECTION

To overcome means to conquer, defeat, overpower, triumph, prevail over, and bring under subjection. Jesus demonstrated the law of reproduction: HE reproduced more disciples like HIMself. HE imparted HIS authority, anointing, glory, power, and wisdom to his disciples in order for them to go into the world and spread the Gospel.

In Matthew 10:1 KJV, states, *"And when HE had called unto HIM HIS twelve disciples, HE gave them power against unclean spirits, to cast them out, and to heal all manner of sickness and all manner of disease".*

Jesus had appointed seventy disciples to go into the world and preach the good news of the Gospel, to save the lost, to deliver, heal and set them free to be new creatures in him, through the confession of their sins and acceptance of Him as Lord and Savior, and the seventy returned with joy, saying, *"Lord, even the devils are subject unto us through thy name!", (*LUKE 10:17 KJV).

The greatest decision I have ever made in my life was to accept the LORDship of JESUS Christ in my life. Through a really deep and intimate relationship with Him, I received His unconditional, agape love. Just like the disciples, He transformed me into an overcomer. That's why I can take authority over the spirit of rejection and live out the plans He has for me, for His Glory. It is my heartfelt prayer that many will do the same. REJECT THE SPIRIT OF REJECTION!

PRAYER OF DELIVERANCE FROM THE SPIRIT OF REJECTION

In the name of JESUS, I renounce the spirit of rejection that seeks to operate in my life. With my GOD- given authority and the faith that I possess, I render this spirit powerless and inoperable forever!

I uproot and dismantle all plots and schemes assigned to disrupt the plans and purposes my HEAVENLY FATHER has for me. I forgive my family members and ancestors that may have passed this spirit to me generationally.

I renounce and reject all forms of the spirit of rejection, which includes fear of rejection, inherited rejection, parental rejection, perceived rejection, self-rejection, and societal rejection.

In the name of JESUS, I radically and swiftly close every door against the spirit of rejection and cancel every legal right and access that this spirit has on my life.

I command all forms of rejection to lose their hold on me now, in JESUS' name. I welcome and accept the LOVE of JESUS and all that HE has for me throughout eternity by faith.

With this LOVE and ACCEPTANCE in CHRIST JESUS, I breakthrough and decree and declare that I will move forward in obedience, faith, love, dominion, power, and wisdom, and receive my KINGLY inheritance! My HEAVENLY FATHER is KING of

KINGS and LORD of LORDS and HIS KINGDOM reigns over my life forever!!!

OVERCOMING
THE SPIRIT OF THE REJECTION

Scriptures on GOD's LOVE AND ACCEPTANCE

1)   Deuteronomy 31:8 KJV
"And the Lord, HE it is that doth go before thee; HE will be with thee, HE will not fail thee, neither forsake thee: fear not, neither be dismayed".

2)   Psalm 27:10 KJV
"When my father and my mother forsake me, then the LORD will take me up".

3)   Psalm 139: 13, 14 KJV
"For thou hast possessed my reins: thou hast covered me in my mother's womb".
"I will praise thee; for I am fearfully and wonderfully made: marvelous are thy works; and that my soul knoweth right well".

4)   John 3:16 *KJV*

"For GOD so loved the world, that HE gave HIS only begotten SON, that whosoever believeth in HIM should not perish, but have everlasting life".

    5)   John 6:37 KJV

"All that the FATHER giveth me shall come to me; and HIM that cometh to me I will in no wise cast out".

    6)   Romans 8:1 *KJV*

"There is therefore now no condemnation to them which are in CHRIST JESUS, who walk not after the flesh, but after the SPIRIT".

    7)   Romans 8:15 *KJV*

"For ye have not received the spirit of bondage again to fear; but ye have received the SPIRIT of ADOPTION, whereby we cry, ABBA, FATHER".

    8)   Galatians 2:20 *KJV*

"I am crucified with CHRIST: nevertheless, I live; yet not I, but CHRIST liveth in me: and the life which I now live in the flesh I live by the faith of the SON of GOD, who loved me, and gave HIMSELF for me".

    9)   Ephesians 1:5, 6 *KJV*

"Having predestined us unto the adoption of children by JESUS CHRIST to HIMSELF, according to the good

pleasure of HIS will, To the praise of the glory of HIS grace, wherein HE hath made us accepted in the beloved".

    10)   Ephesians 2:10 *KJV*

"For we are HIS workmanship, created in CHRIST JESUS unto good works, which GOD hath before ordained that we should walk in them".

ABOUT THE AUTHOR

Dr. Vivian Carroll, Ph.D. is a wife, mother, pastor, N.Y.S Chaplain, teacher, counselor and life coach. Dr. Vivian Carroll has been a N.Y.C teacher for the Department of Education since 1988. She began working in the field as a special educator for home-bound students in 2002. Because she has taught many students who were very ill, she developed a heartfelt passion to see many lives set free through the power of God. She is one of the many prophetic voices in this hour that has been raised up to minister healing and deliverance to the hurting and the lost.

In 2007, God developed another passion in her heart. This time it was for women. She encountered women for all walks of life that needed emotional and mental healing etc. They needed those that would be compassionate enough to hear their hearts' cry as wives, mothers, and as women living and working in every day society. Dr. Carroll founded Brides for Christ International Women's Ministry.

In 2014 Dr. Vivian Carroll became CEO of Carroll Enterprise, LLC, her family-owned business. Alongside her husband, Apostle Stanley Carroll, she pastors Purple Heart Ministries, International, in Danbury, Ct. Their adult sons, Jahrell and Jamel Carroll co-labors with them.

Made in the USA
Coppell, TX
22 September 2023

21892648R00026